MEALTIME
WORDS

Jenny Tyler
Illustrated by Sue Stitt

With consultant advice from John Newson and Gillian Hartley of the Child Development Research Unit at Nottingham University, and Robyn Gee.

Designed by Kim Blundell and Mary Cartwright

biscuit

spoon

apple

bowl

ice cream

bib

cake

cup

egg

banana

apple

ice cream

cake

bib

spoon

egg

cup

bowl

biscuit

banana